Dedication

This book is dedicated to all children who are sad, lonely, or who need a friend.

Copyright

©Copyright 2025 George Baron and Deb Pickering. All Rights Reserved. It is illegal to reproduce, duplicate and transmit any part of this document in either electronic mean or printed format. Recording of this publication is strictly prohibited.

THE DRAGON THUNDER

Three little dragons love to spend their school holidays in the Dragon Park, in the sky. One day a big angry dragon arrives and starts throwing the equipment around. This really scares the little dragons. But then, being very brave, they try to find out what is making him so angry…
This delightful little story, about loneliness and kindness, was first written by George when he was 6.
We hope you enjoy reading it as much as we've enjoyed writing it.

Once upon a time there was a baby dragon, called Happy. He had 2 best friends called Super and Miles. They liked to play in the Dragon Park.

The Dragon Park was in the sky, because of course: all dragons can fly!
They loved it too, that, because all the equipment was in the clouds, it kept moving around! That made it much more fun!

The dragon slide was Happy's favourite because it was amazingly long and when Happy got to the bottom of the slide, he could fly back up to the top.

Miles loved the roller-coaster, because it was 'speedy-fast'.
But Super loved the tea-cups, because he said they were, "Spinny-spinny!"

One day, a big angry dragon came into the Dragon Park and he started throwing the equipment everywhere. The three little dragons were very scared and they hid behind the tea cups. Happy looked over a cup and said, "Why are you throwing all the equipment around?"

"I feel angry ALL THE TIME and nothing seems to make it go away. I'm so stompy and loud and everybody is frightened of me." The big dragon replied, plonking himself down on a park bench. "I've got no friends."

Miles, who was the really thoughtful one of the three friends, looked at the big dragon, from behind his tea-cup and asked quietly, "Do you know why you feel angry all the time?"

"Not really," answered the big dragon, "My mum and dad have gone to work abroad, and I've got to live with my gran and grandad. I love them but I don't feel like they like having me around much.
Gran goes to knitting club all the time and Grandad goes to the pub and plays darts. But I can't go to swimming or running club anymore because they're too busy to take me.
I have to go straight home from school, and do my homework, and I'm not allowed to go to friends' houses or bring friends to gran's house."

His eyes filled with tears. "I feel really really lonely and angry that nobody seems to understand how I feel."

"Woah," said Super. That seemed like a lot!

The baby dragons came out from behind the tea-cups, and sat on each side of the big dragon, on the park bench.

"You know," said Happy, "When my gran died, my mum said she felt exactly like that! She said she thought she should be sad but instead she just felt angry and resentful ALL the time."

"Really?" asked the big dragon looking at Happy hopefully.

"Yeah really." Happy nodded. "One day, I dropped a few beans on the carpet, and usually Mum would just shake her head and get a cloth to clean it up, but this day she really 'flipped-her-stack'!" Happy shuddered at the thought.

"Did she hurt you?" asked the big dragon.

"Oh no, nothing like that. She would NEVER do that. But she really shouted and was angry for ages. Then she came to me afterwards and said she was sorry about being angry all the time…" Happy trailed off.

"So maybe what you're feeling is normal?" added Miles.

"I'm Happy, by the way, and this is Super and Miles." Happy said pointing to his friends as he said their names. "What are you called?"

"Luis" the big dragon sniffed.

"Hiya Luis" The three baby dragons said together.

"We can be your friends, if you'd like?" Happy said, looking at his friends to make sure they were OK with that. They both nodded.

"Yes please." Said Luis, wiping his eyes with the back of his big paw.

Then Happy pointed at the mess, "Why don't you help us put the equipment back, and we can all play together?"
"Yeah," said Super, "All four of us can play together."

Together the four dragons began to tidy up. At one point, Super was really struggling to turn over the tea-cups that had been tipped over.

"I can help," said Luis and quickly went beside Super to help tip the cups back the right way up.

"Thanks Luis," smiled Super, "It's always easier to do things as a thunder."

"What does that mean?" Luis asked as he flapped his wings gently to keep him in one place.

"A team, or a group of dragons is called a thunder, because that's how it sounds when we're all flying together." Super grinned, showing his white pointy teeth.

Luis grinned back, "I like being part of your thunder."

"We like it too," Happy grinned, looking round and realising, with relief, that together they had tidied everything back into place.

"Race you to the slide," Happy shouted as he laughed and quickly flew off.

They all laughed and flew to the slide, then went down the slide one after the other. And that was just the start of this thunder's adventures.

About the Authors

George and his nana (Deb Pickering) live on the outskirts of York and have been making stories up together since George was old enough to talk. They could spend hours making a story up and acting it out: Deb remembers one afternoon in particular when George's teddy, Froggy, ended up falling down a deep well – over and over – and George had to come up with new ways to get Froggy out!

Dragon Thunder was a story that Deb encouraged George to write when he was 6. Recently, when Deb was getting some other work published, she suggested George might like to get this book published too. They worked on it together after that: And here it is!

www.ingramcontent.com/pod-product-compliance
Lightning Source LLC
Chambersburg PA
CBHW041121070526
44584CB00002B/229